Other titles in the series:

KT-387-351

LIBRARIES NI
WITHDRAWN FROM STOCK

978 1 4451 4166 4

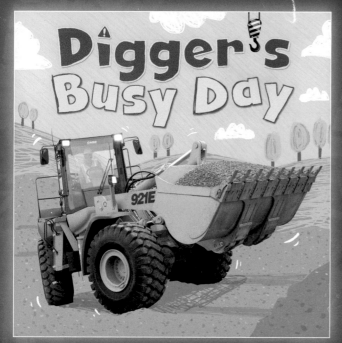

978 1 4451 4311 8

978 1 4451 4319 4

www.franklinwatts.co.uk

Franklin Watts
First published in Great Britain in 2015 by The Watts Publishing Group

Copyright © The Watts Publishing Group

All rights reserved.

Picture credits: ChameleonsEye/Shutterstock: 22-23; Dobresum/Shutterstock: 4bl, 14-15, 29r; Paul Drabot/Shutterstock: 12-13; Flying Colours/Getty Images: front cover; Andrew Holt/Getty Images: 3, 5b, 8-9, 28br; V S Luma/Shutterstock: 4cr, 26-27, 28cr; nicolamargaret/istockphoto: back cover, 24-25; Sue Robinson/Shutterstock: 5c, 20-21, 29l; Shane Shaw/istockphoto: 4br, 6-7, 28bl; Twigra/Shutterstock: 10-11; VanderWolf Images/Shutterstock: 16-17; Dmitry Vereschagin/Shutterstock: 18-19.

Editor: Melanie Palmer
Designer & Illustrator: Dan Bramall
Design Manager: Peter Scoulding
Picture researcher: Diana Morris

Every attempt has been made to clear copyright. Should there be any inadvertent omission please apply to the publisher for rectification.

HB ISBN 978 1 4451 4315 6
PB ISBN 978 1 4451 4316 3
Library ebook ISBN 978 1 4451 4318 7

Printed in China

Franklin Watts
An imprint of
Hachette Children's Group
Part of The Watts Publishing Group
Carmelite House
50 Victoria Embankment
London EC4Y 0DZ

An Hachette UK Company
www.hachette.co.uk

www.franklinwatts.co.uk

MIX
Paper from
responsible sources
FSC® C104740
FSC
www.fsc.org

Emergency!
Emergency!

Written by Amelia Marshall

Illustrated by Dan Bramall

W
FRANKLIN WATTS
LONDON•SYDNEY

Flashing lights and sirens wail — NEE NAW! NEE NAW! NEE NAW!

The vehicles get ready with a **ROAR, ROAR, ROAR!**

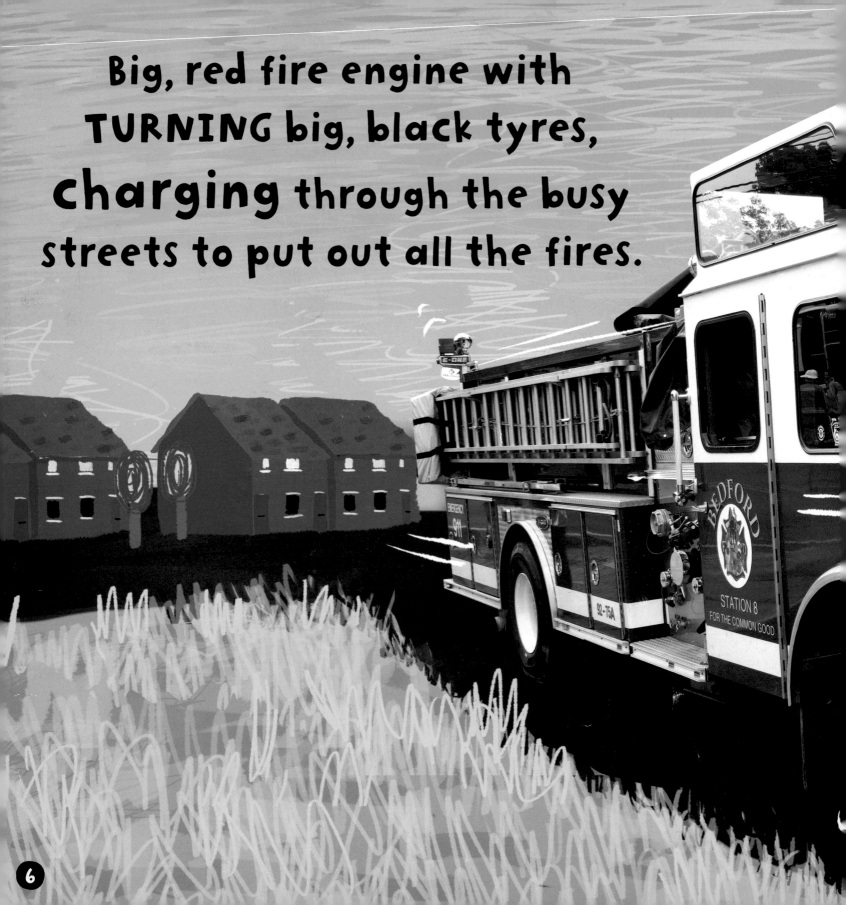

Big, red fire engine with TURNING big, black tyres, charging through the busy streets to put out all the fires.

Police car **SCREECHES,**
the sirens blare away.
EMERGENCY! EMERGENCY!
Make way! Make way!

Speedy police bike
ZIPPING really fast,
ZIG-ZAG ZAGGING
with blue lights flashing past.

Quick! Quick!
The rescue plane is RACING through the sky,

115462

climbing through the clouds, flying way up high!

Airport fire rescue truck is waiting on standby, **HEAVING** hefty water tanks while all the planes fly by.

Snow rescue vehicle
CHUGS across the **Snow**,
pushing through the ice,
Hurry! Hurry! Go!

Creak, creak, groan!
Rescue truck is ready.
HEAVE HO, HEAVE HO,
steady, steady, steady!

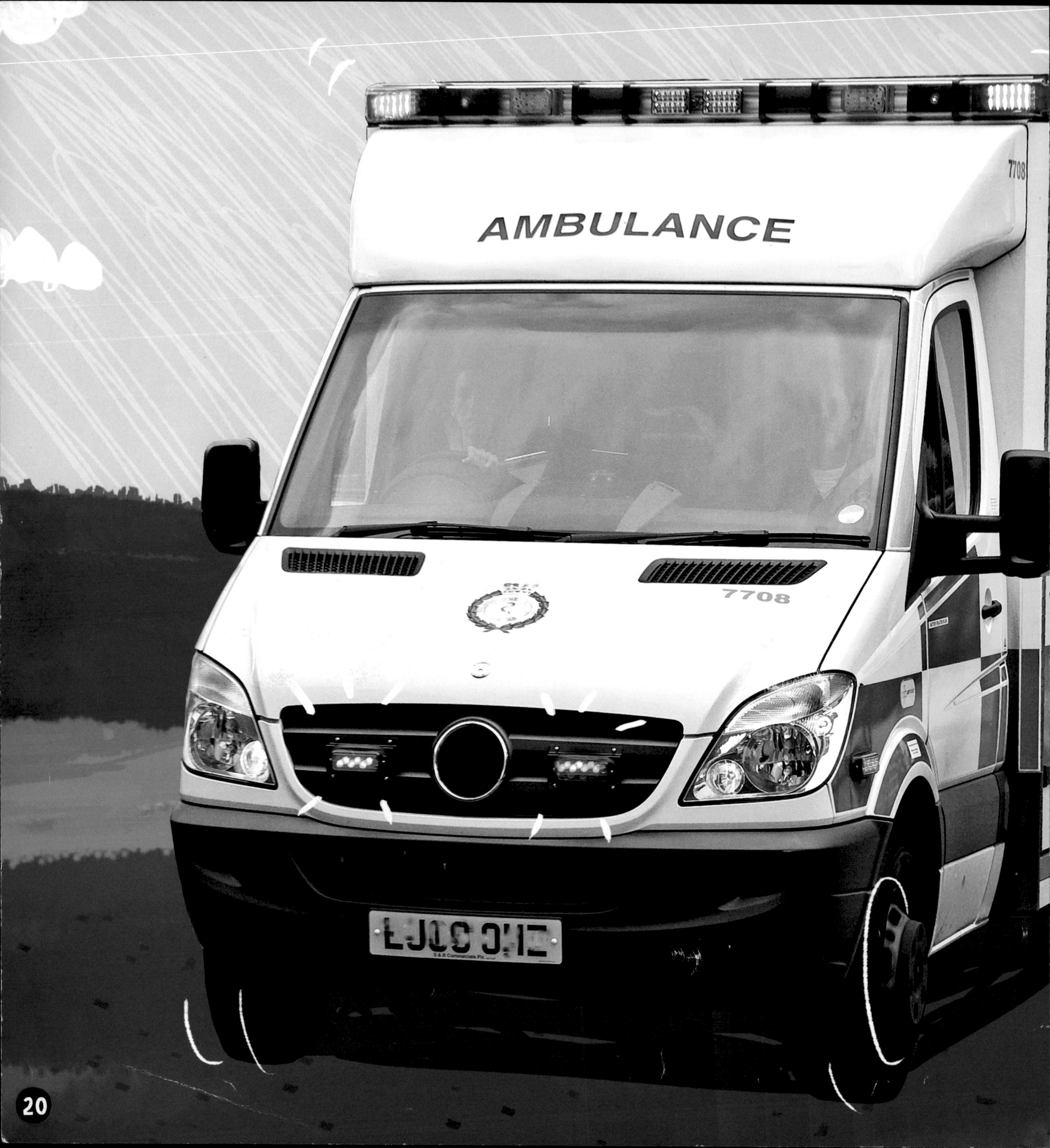
AMBULANCE
7708

NEE NAW! NEE NAW!
Blue lights are **FLASHING.**
Hurry out the way,
the **ambulance** is dashing.

Lifeguard van is on patrol **UP** and **down** the beach.

Driving over sand and surf, **no one** is out of reach!

Lifeboat to the rescue!
CRASH! CRASH! CRASH!
Jumping over bumpy waves,

Splish! Splash! Splash!

Chugga! Chugga! Chugga!

Big propellers chopping!

Helicopter hovers —

it rescues without stopping!

Now all is safe and all is calm,
the emergencies are done.

The sirens slowly stop their noise, lights out now, one by one.

Emergency terms

 **Siren** – loud sound to warn people to move out of the way.

Propellers – blades that go round to help a helicopter or plane lift up.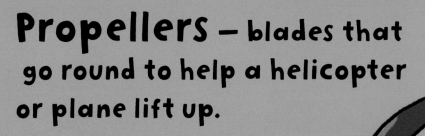

Ladder – helps firefighters to reach tall buildings.

Hose – a tube that carries water, used to fight fires.

Wings – help a plane to lift and fly.

Motor – machine that supplies power to a vehicle to make it move.

Crane – a machine that helps lift heavy loads.

Tyres – cover wheels so they can grip the road.